Talking to God

A Child's Guide to Prayer

MARILYN J. WOODY
ILLUSTRATED BY KAY SALEM

A Faith Parenting Guide can be found on page 32.

Dedicated to:

Richard, the prayer partner God gave me.

*"To clasp the hands in prayer is the beginning
of an uprising against the disorder of the world."*

Karl Barth, Theologian

Acknowledgments

Special thanks to critique group members:

Debbie Alten, Irene Faubion, Arleta Richardson, Sharon Pearson,
Brenda Powell, Jane Rumph, Lisa Saint, and Pat Verbal.

And grateful acknowledgment to the teachers, moms,
and children who gave valuable advice.

And all who prayed.

Faith Kids™ is an imprint of
Cook Communications Ministries, Colorado Springs, CO 80918
Cook Communications, Paris, Ontario
Kingsway Communications, Eastbourne, England

TALKING TO GOD
© 2000 by Marilyn J. Woody for text and Kay Salem for illustrations.

Edited by Liz Duckworth
Designed by Pamela Poll Graphic Design
First printing, 2000
Printed in China
04 03 02 01 00 5 4 3 2 1

Table of Contents

"If Solomon was the wisest man who ever lived, then why did he need to pray?"

Solomon was the wisest, richest, and most respected king who ever lived. When he became king, God told Solomon he could ask for anything and God would give it to him.

Solomon wanted to be a good leader so he asked God to make him wise. God was happy about his request. God said He would make Solomon not only wise but also rich and honorable.

Did Solomon say to himself, "Since I'm so wise and rich and famous, now I don't need to pray?"

The Bible says no.

In fact, Solomon prayed to God asking Him to always hear and answer his prayers. Solomon thanked God for keeping His promises.

The wisest and richest man who ever lived knew he needed God and prayed to Him. If God said you could ask for one of the following, which would you choose? To be brave or a good friend, or perhaps to always be honest or kind to others? God is pleased when we ask for things like that.

See 2 Chronicles 1–7.

Dear God,
Help me to remember I always need You
with me. I need You more than money or
being famous. Amen.

"You are the God
who keeps his kind
promises to all those
who obey you, and
who are anxious to
do your will."

2 Chronicles 6:14, TLB

5

"What can I say when I don't know how to pray?"

If a dog is chasing you or a big kid says, "Wanna fight?" you can probably think of something to pray about! Or maybe you're worried about your spelling test or soccer game. When big people pray, they sound so good. It seems like they know just the right words to use.

But sometimes you don't know what to say to God. You may feel sad, mad, lonely, or scared. Is there still a way to pray?

The Bible says yes.

God talks to us through the Bible. We talk to Him through our prayers. But when you can't put your feelings into words, God says the Holy Spirit speaks for you. He knows what you're thinking and tells God. What a great plan! Isn't that strong power?

See Romans 8.

"For we don't even know what we should pray for . . . but the Holy Spirit prays for us with such feeling that it cannot be expressed in words."

Romans 8:26, TLB

Dear God,
Thank You for knowing when
I can't think of the right words
to say to You. I'm glad You
hear me anyway. Amen.

6

"Am I supposed to pray for our president and other leaders?"

Can your prayers cause leaders to think about God? If you prayed for them each day, would it really make any difference? Can kids do anything to help solve problems? Could your city or town or home ever live in peace?

    The Bible says yes.

God tells us to pray every day for our leaders. That means our president, judges, mayors, police officers, and fire fighters. Also our parents, friends, pastor, and teachers. If these people are obeying God, He says our lives will be peaceful and quiet.

What bothers you about where you live? People who are mean or fighting, or things that aren't fair? Maybe you are worried about some of these things today. The good news is that prayer causes God's power to work.

See 1 Timothy 2:1-6.

Dear God,
I want to live where it is
safe and peaceful. Thank You
for our leaders. Help them to
be honest and fair. Amen.

"Pray in this way for kings and all others who are in authority over us . . . so that we can live in peace and quietness."

1 Timothy 2:2, TLB

9

"Will God answer my prayer to protect me from the devil?"

"My prayer is not that you take them out of the world but that you protect them from the evil one."

John 17:15, NIV

You may have watched TV today. Sometimes things you watch scare you. So many bad things happen in the world it makes you want to pull the blankets over your head at night and pretend they're not real.

Does God know about the stuff on TV or when you're tempted to do wrong things?

The Bible says yes.

God knows about the bad news. He knows when you start to say unkind things about others or don't want to obey your parents or begin to cheat in school. He tells us to pray each day for our protection from evil.

Prayer can help you do what's right. Instead of waiting until you get in trouble, God wants you to know about your enemy, the devil, and pray for protection. He helps us not to be afraid. God says the enemy runs at the sound of His voice. Isn't that powerful?

See John 17.

Dear God,
Please keep me from the evil one.
Help me to want to do what's right.
Thanks for being such a powerful God! Amen.

"Can prayer help to keep me from doing wrong things?"

When people fight a war they plan whether to use laser weapons, guns, bombs, or missiles. They want whatever will kill, defeat, or hurt the enemy.

Our enemy is the evil one known as the devil. He tries to make us do wrong things. Is there some way to be safe from him?

The Bible says yes.

God has a great plan to defeat the devil. He tells us in the Bible how we can put on our armor and stand strong. To help you remember to do this, you can imagine putting on your armor piece by piece when you dress each morning.

First, pray for the *belt of truth* around your waist. Now, fasten the *breast-plate of righteousness* to protect your heart. Hold your foot up and pray on the *shoes of peace*.

Take the *shield of faith* to stop the arrows of the evil one. Stick the *helmet of salvation* on your head and then pull out the *sword of the Spirit* which is God's Word, the Bible. There you are, dressed in God's armor with His mighty power all around you.

See Ephesians 6:10-20.

Dear God,
Thanks for being more powerful than
the devil. Help me to remember to put
on my armor each day. I pray to be
kept safe from the evil one. Amen.

"The weapons we fight with are not the weapons of the world. On the contrary, they have divine power to demolish strongholds."

2 Corinthians 10:4, NIV

"Should I pray for someone who has hurt me?"

Kids can be really mean to each other. Maybe a friend or your brother or sister hurt you. Or perhaps somebody at school didn't ask you to join in a game or eat lunch. Has anyone ever made you feel so bad that you hoped they would hurt too? You may want to pay them back for being unkind.

Does God know and care how we feel when our hurts make us angry?

The Bible says yes.

A young man named Joseph had brothers who were really mean to him. They sold him to some men who took him to Egypt. The brothers told their father that Joseph was killed by a wild animal.

God was with Joseph, though. God not only rescued Joseph from his troubles, but the king of Egypt trusted him so much he put Joseph in charge of the whole country! Years later, the people in Joseph's old land began running out of food, so his brothers went to Egypt to find some. Imagine how surprised they were to see their own brother giving out the food!

Now Joseph had a chance to get back at his brothers. Instead he chose to forgive them. God's power can help us let go of our anger and hurt against those who are unkind to us. God turned Joseph's brothers' evil deeds into good. What amazing power!

See Genesis 37–50.

Dear God,
Thanks for knowing how I feel when
somebody is unkind to me. Help me
to choose to forgive. I love You. Amen.

"Make sure that nobody pays back wrong for wrong, but always try to be kind to each other and to everyone else."

1 Thessalonians 5:15, NIV

15

"Does God even read mail? Could I write to Him?"

Tommy heard his mom and dad talking. "The man at the garage says we need new brakes on the car, but we don't have enough money," his dad said as he showed Tommy's mom the bill.

"Since we need good brakes to be safe, maybe we should lay the bill on the table and pray over it," Tommy's mom said. "I was just reading in the Bible that when a king named Hezekiah had a big problem, he spread out a letter before God. Then God took care of the need." So Tommy's family placed the bill on the kitchen table and prayed.

Does God really care about things like car brakes?

The Bible says yes.

Imagine how excited Tommy and his family were when they received a letter in the mail from his grandparents. It said, "We had a yard sale last week. As we prayed about what to do with the money, we felt we should send part of it to you." The check was for the exact amount of the car repair bill!

God wants us to tell Him our needs. We never know how He may show His power in our lives.

See 2 Kings 18 and 19.

Dear God,
Thanks for caring about all my needs,
and for hearing my prayers just like You
did Hezekiah's. Amen.

"Then [Hezekiah] went up to the temple of the Lord and spread [the letter] out before the Lord."

2 Kings 19:14, NIV

17

Chores
• feed dog
• make bed
• clean mirror
• take out trash

"Will I always get what I want if I pray?"

Allison had chores to do each day. She was supposed to make her bed, take out the trash, and feed her dog, Lizzy. If she forgot to do one of her jobs, and her mom reminded her, sometimes she whined or complained.

"I know chores aren't fun, and you may not want to do them, but we all need to work together in our home," her mom told her. "Your jobs won't seem so bad if you have a good attitude, and life will be better for all of us."

Does a good attitude and cooperation help you know better how to pray or obey the commandment to, "Honor your father and mother"?

The Bible says yes.

God wants us to pray for His will instead of demanding our own way to get what we want. When we believe that our parents know what is good for us, we understand better how to pray. Sometimes what we think we want will not be best for us, and God knows that. When we pray, "Your will be done," it tells God we trust Him with our lives.

See Matthew 26:36-46.

Father God,
When I pray, I have my own ideas
about how I want You to answer. Help
me to want Your will and to trust
that You know what's best for me. Amen.

". . . your will be done."

Matthew 26:42, NIV

"Is there only one person who hears and answers prayer?"

A wicked king named Ahab hated the prophet Elijah, because Elijah trusted God and prayed only to Him. Ahab and his 450 prophets prayed to Baal, a pretend god made of stone.

Elijah told Ahab he would prove who the true God was. Each man stacked up wood with an animal sacrifice on it. Elijah said to Ahab, "Call on the name of your god, but do not light the fire." The prophets yelled and yelled to Baal. They jumped and danced around the altar. Nothing happened.

Elijah teased them saying, "Shout louder! Surely he is a god. Maybe he's thinking, or traveling, or sleeping." Still, nothing happened.

Then Elijah had his helpers pour four large jars of water over the wood on the altar to the living God. They did this three times until the wood was soaking wet. Elijah prayed, "O Lord, answer me, so these people will know You are the true, living God." Do you think God heard Elijah?

The Bible says yes.

Then the fire of the Lord fell from above and burned up the sacrifice, the wood, the stones, the dirt, and the water! This happened because of God's power. When the people saw this they cried, "The Lord, He is God!"

See 1 Kings 18.

Strong God,
Help me to never pray to anyone but You. I want to
see Your mighty power at work. Amen.

"O Lord, hear me praying . . . for I will never pray to anyone but you."

Psalm 5:2, TLB

21

"Can I pray to be strong and mighty?"

"I bet I'm stronger than you! See my muscles? See, I can jump higher."

Do you dream of being strong and mighty? TV ads say you can be powerful if you eat certain cereals or jump higher if you wear the right tennis shoes. Maybe you wish you were like Batman or Superman. Does God have a way for you to be strong and brave?

The Bible says yes.

God doesn't need magic shoes or secret formulas. God has something even better. He knows how you can become strong and brave in hard or even impossible situations. That's what a man named Peter did.

Wicked King Herod was killing people who loved God. He put Peter in jail overnight, planning to kill him the next day. Peter was handcuffed between two soldiers, and guards also stood at the jail gates. Herod was taking no chances that Peter would escape.

Surprise! God sent one of His mighty angels to rescue Peter. They slipped out of the jail without the guards even seeing them. Peter went straight to the home of friends who had prayed all night for his safety. When they saw him they went wild! He told them how God had released him from jail. Once again, God showed His mighty power as people prayed.

See Acts 12.

> *Dear God,*
> *Thank You for being so big and strong*
> *and mighty that You can do anything. Amen.*

"[Peter] went to the house of Mary . . . where many people had gathered and were praying."

Acts 12:12, NIV

"Can God turn bad things into good if I pray?"

A wicked man named Haman wanted to kill all Jewish people, including Queen Esther. God had allowed Esther to become queen so she could help save her people.

When Esther heard about Haman's awful plot to murder all the Jews, she made a plan. First, she asked her family and friends to go without food for three days and to pray to God. Then she invited Haman to a special dinner with her husband, the king. Haman worked for the king, but the king didn't know about the evil thing Haman planned to do.

So right in front of Haman, Queen Esther said to the king, "Would you want to have your queen killed and her people, too?" Then Esther told him what Haman planned to do. The king was furious. He had Haman killed and gave his important job to Esther's uncle, Mordecai, who became a kind and fair ruler. Did God allow this to happen?

The Bible says yes.

When Queen Esther and many other Jews fasted, which means to go without food and pray, God showed His mighty power. Maybe you'll never help save a lot of people like Queen Esther, but you don't know how God may use you when you stand up for Him.

See the Book of Esther.

*Dear God,
Help me to have the same courage and
trust as Queen Esther did. When people
are treated unfairly, I want to help. Amen.*

24

"Is it true God stores my prayers in a golden bowl?"

Dustin prays for his grandma who lives far away. Cassie prays for her sick cat. Taylor tells God he's afraid of the dark. Another kid asks God to help his mom and dad to get along and stop arguing.

How can God listen to so many different prayers and keep them all sorted out? It's hard for us to hear more than one person talk at a time. Can God really hear lots of prayers all at once and answer them?

The Bible says yes.

God knows we might get tired or confused about praying, so He tells us in the Bible how important our prayers are. They are so important that He keeps them along with our praises in a golden bowl. When we talk to God, He says our prayers are like perfume, or a sweet smelling rose. They are God's treasures.

See Revelation 5.

Dear God,
I'm glad You know how to listen to lots of
people all at once and that You treasure my
prayers and praises. Please help me
remember to always say "thank You." Amen.

"Each one had a harp and they were holding golden bowls full of incense, which are the prayers of the saints [God's people]."

Revelation 5:8, NIV

27

"What if people make fun of me when I pray?"

Jehoshaphat, King of Judah, loved God. When another king, Ahab, asked him to help fight some people, Jehoshaphat said, "Let's ask God first."

Ahab and his leaders made fun of the way Jehoshaphat trusted God. Instead of praying to God they took advice from men who hated God. Some of these wicked leaders even declared war on Jehoshaphat and his people. Jehoshaphat was very upset, but his first thought was to ask God for help.

He prayed in front of a large crowd of people, "O God, we have no power to face this huge army that is attacking us. We do not know what to do, but our eyes are upon you."

Do you think God said, "Sorry, you're on your own"?

The Bible says no.

God told Jehoshaphat, "Do not be afraid or discouraged because of this big army. For the battle is not yours, but God's." When they went to war, they discovered God had already fought for them. Not an enemy escaped!

You may have kids in your neighborhood or at school who make fun of you because you love God. Remember, God is like a strong tower.

See 2 Chronicles 20:1-30.

Dear God,
I want my friends to like me. If they
make fun of me because I love You, help
me to remember You know what's going on
and will help me to be brave. Amen.

"He alone is my rock and my salvation; he is my fortress, I will not be shaken."

Psalm 62:6, NIV

28

"Does God want me to pray if I've been bad?"

Saul hated people who loved God. He would arrest them and drag them to jail. One day he was suddenly struck by a bright light that left him blind. A voice said, "Saul, Saul, why are you out to get me?"

Saul said, "Who's talking to me?"

"I am Jesus, the one you're hunting down," came the answer. "Go to the next city and wait," Jesus said to Saul. The men with him led him to the nearby city. For three days Saul was blind and didn't eat or drink anything.

Jesus told another man, Ananias, to go to Saul. Ananias told Saul how he could stop being mean and wicked and learn to love God. Do you think Saul believed him?

> The Bible says yes.

Saul could suddenly see again and became a man who loved Jesus with all his heart. Saul followed Jesus the rest of his life. God gave him a clean heart and a new name, Paul.

Do you ever feel you've been so bad God doesn't want to hear your voice? That's exactly when He wants to hear from you. God is able to change lives. You may want to pray this prayer to Him:

See Acts 9:1-28.

Dear Jesus,
Forgive me for the wrong things I've done.
Thank You for loving me. Please come into
my life, and help me to follow You every day. Amen.

"Create in me a new, clean heart, O God, filled with clean thoughts and right desires."

Psalm 51:10, TLB

31

Talking to God

Ages: 4-7

Life Issue: I want my child to understand the power of prayer.

Spiritual Building Block: Prayer

Learning Styles

Sight: Help your child to collect prayer requests in a "golden bowl" which you can make together out of paper plates. Cut a paper plate in half and staple the sides together. You could cover the plate with gold-foil wrapping paper to compete the effect. Help your child write prayer requests on slips of paper to keep in the "bowl." Take one out each morning and pray for that need together.

Sound: Memorize 1 Thessalonians 5:15, "Make sure that nobody pays back wrong for wrong, but always try to be kind to each other and to everyone else." Talk about what it means to pay back "wrong for wrong." Ask if your child can remember a time when he or she wanted to get back at someone after being hurt. Then make a list of people that you can each show kindness to.

Touch: Help your child make a "whole armor of God" costume. You could use cardboard, shoe boxes, an old belt, and worn-out slippers or boots. Cover cut-out pieces with foil to create a helmet, sword, breastplate, shoes, etc. Talk about what each piece of armor means. Read aloud Ephesians 6:10-20 and encourage your child to put on each piece as you read about it.